ELDERS
OF THE
FAITHS

Interviews and Portraits
by
Mark W. McGinnis

Ex Machina Publishing Company
Sioux Falls, SD
1996

Copyright © 1996 by Mark W. McGinnis

Published by Ex Machina Publishing Company
Box 448
Sioux Falls, SD 57101

First Printing, July 1996

Library of Congress Cataloging-in-Publication Data

McGinnis, Mark W., 1950-
  Elders of the faiths : interviews and portraits / by Mark W.
McGinnis.
    p.   cm.
  Includes bibliographical references (p.).
  ISBN 0-944287-15-8 (trade pbk.)
    1. South Dakota--Religion--20th century. 2. Religious
biography--South Dakota---Interviews.   I. Title.
  BL2527.S8M34 1996
  200'.92'2783--dc20   96-16553
                                                             CIP

ISBN 0-944287-15-8 (Paper Trade)

*dedicated to three elders
dear to my heart*

my mother
Irene McGinnis

and my in-laws
Bud and Eunice Pirnie

The author would like to express his sincere appreciation to to South Dakota Peace and Justice Center director, board, and general membership for their assistance with the **Elders of the Faiths** project.

South Dakota Peace and Justice Center
P.O. Box 405
Watertown, South Dakota, 57201
605-882-2822

ELDERS OF THE FAITHS

Artist's Statement

Since 1992 I have been working on a series of large canvases and essays titled *Designs of Faith*. The series is a study of world religions with an emphasis on their philosophy, morals, and foundational history. At the half way point of this project, in the summer of 1995, I decided to take a break from my studies and pursue the same subject from a more personal perspective. I resolved to do a series of interviews and portraits of elders belonging to some of the religions of the region where I live.

To help me select the participants in the project, I turned to the members of the South Dakota Peace and Justice Center, with whom I have been long associated. The Center put out a call to their members for nominations for the project and received over fifty marvelous nominees. From this group the SDPJC Board of Directors helped me edit the list to the fifteen elders who were invited to participate.

From January of 1995 through the early summer I traveled the region interviewing and photographing the elders. It is impossible to express in written form the depth of the experiences. The landscapes, the communities, the homes, the families, the kindness and hospitality of the elders were learning experiences on many levels. I used a standard set of questions in the interviews though occasionally I omitted one or more.

The written product from the interview was a distillation of hours of conversation that many times meandered in multiple interesting directions. My first drafts of the interviews were edited by the former director of SDPJC, Legia Spicer, and the current director, Jeanne Koster. Their guidance greatly improved the written component. The interviews were lastly reviewed by the elders themselves, making certain I was correctly reflecting their thoughts.

The portraits were painted in the summer of 1995 using photos and notes from the interview sessions as sources. I would many times combine various aspects of different photos of an elder to create an image I felt better reflected the character I wished to convey. The portraits are not meant to be a photographic likeness of the elder. Had I wished that

v

effect I would have used photographs. Instead I wanted to use the emphasis of texture, color, and line that is part of my painting technique to create an interpretation of the elder. I found painting the portraits just as rewarding an experience as doing the interviews. My subjects had a tremendous variety of facial qualities enhanced by the details of the many decades of living. The cloud pattern in the background of each portrait is based on the sky the day of the interview.

Doing these portraits led me to contemplate what I would call "the aesthetics of age." We live in a society that puts prime value on youth and the visual beauty of youth. The desirability of youth is constantly marketed to us in obvious and subtle ways. It has been said that if an American has just turned fifty years old and mentions it to a friend, the friend may well respond, "You don't look a day over forty!" In traditional China, in the same situation, when the Chinese mentions turning fifty the friend might respond, "Oh, you look at least sixty!" Both friends are attempting to be kind but in traditional China it is positive to look old.

I believe there is an aesthetic - a type of beauty - to aging. The study involved in doing these portraits certainly helped to reinforce this belief. As we age we physically change. It is a natural process: lines deepen, hair color changes, sometimes even eye color and skin color change, shapes and forms change. These changes reflect not the tight, smooth beauty of youth, but another kind of beauty of texture and line. They are a beauty reflecting time, a beauty reflecting character, and can be a beauty reflecting wisdom. I hope my portraits convey some of that aesthetic.

As I look on this project with its diverse and thoughtful faces and words, I feel fortunate to have had the experience. I also think of the thirty-five nominees who were not interviewed and painted. I also think of elders who are all around us — in the grocery store, at the movie, walking on the street, at the doctor's office, in our immediate families. There is so much to be learned from our elders in religious matters and all aspects of life. We simply need a small amount of wisdom ourselves to have the sense to ask them.

Mark W. McGinnis
Professor of Art, Northern State University

vi

CONTENTS

Participants

ELDERS OF THE FAITHS

"I hope daily for more awakening to understand the power that lies within us. There is so much we have yet to learn of each individual's potential and how to release it."
— *Beryl Blake*

BERYL BLAKE

born 1911

Beryl Blake has been a member of the Methodist Church all her adult life. She had a long career as a social worker with an emphasis in child welfare and is now retired in Watertown, South Dakota.

Question: *What is your spiritual tradition and how does it form a foundation for your life?*

Answer: I grew up in a very spiritual home. My family had their own ideas, but they also had a sense of tolerance of other ideas as well. It was the horse and buggy days and we had pastors that came out from town to preach in our school on Sundays. We would have a variety of ministers of various denominations that would preach to us. We would go to church no matter which preacher was there. My parents felt we were in need of spiritual guidance and were very uncritical of the ministers. My parents would say when they did not agree with the pastors but they were careful never to put them down in front of the children. They would explain why they didn't agree, but they would make it clear that their disagreement did not make the minister wrong, as everyone has the right to their own beliefs. My mother was a Baptist and my father was a Methodist. Later in my childhood, Mother even taught Sunday school in both churches. Sometimes they would go to services at the Baptist church, sometimes at the Methodist church. We children were allowed to go to whichever church we wanted, and we were not baptized until we were adolescents and could understand what baptism meant. My parents, through my religious traditions, taught me to accept people where they are.

Q. *How has your religion and religious practice given meaning to your life?*

A: My religion is the core of my life. Religion is the center and creates meaning in what I have planned for my life. God as the Holy Spirit is my guide in this planning. God is my center, and to me God is a spirit and not a being. I don't know if God is a he or a she and I don't care. Too many people get hung up on little things when it comes to religion and miss the more important matters. I need the community of the church. I need the strength of the group and the support of people that I know will stand by me.

Q: *What do you believe are the most important values to uphold and promote?*

A: Which values I think are the most important would change depending on which day you might ask me. Today I might say integrity. But then I think of all the white lies I have told to spare others' feelings — that's not integrity, but maybe it is. Another important value is openness, but then I think that openness is a value only to a certain point. Minds must be open to solve problems, but there is also merit in some firmness of beliefs. Patience is another important virtue, but again how far do you go?

Q: *What has given you the most joy in your life?*

A: I have been given great joy in my life by the love of family and friends and people in general, and I interpret that as the love of God coming through them. I also received much happiness through my work as I always loved my work. When I think of the afterlife and think of some people's description of heaven as doing nothing! — I don't think its going to be that way. I hope we will have things to do; we will continue to be productive.

Beryl Blake

Q: *What are your hopes for the future?*

A: I hope daily for more awakening to understand the power that lies within us. There is so much we have yet to learn of each individual's potential and how to release it.

Q: *If there was one thing you could communicate to youth, what would it be?*

A: Unless the youth ask for advice, I wouldn't give it. Young people don't learn from what you tell them; they learn from your actions. If anyone would ask me, I would first say, "Be kind." I feel that young people don't think often enough of the consequences of their actions. We as parents are often too protective. If a youngster should climb a tree, fall and break an arm it will mend. It is better to break an arm than to be afraid to reach for challenges.

"Some people seem too busy trying to impress their neighbors when they should be trying to impress their children. We need real homes for our children — homes of care, love, and discipline."

— *Ted Blakey*

TED BLAKEY
born 1925

Ted Blakey has been a life-long member of the African Methodist Episcopal Church. He has been a businessman in Yankton, South Dakota, where he worked concurrent careers in janitorial service, pest control, and as a bail bondsman. He is now semi-retired.

Question: *What is your spiritual tradition and how does it form a foundation for your life?*

Answer: I grew up in a family of eleven children and we were taught the Golden Rule — do unto others as you would have them do unto you. My father used to say that without discipline you have nothing. I have grown up with these ideas as the basis of my life. I have found that these two things, discipline and love for others in your heart, is all you really need.

Q: *How has your religion and religious practice given meaning to your life?*

A: My religion is everything to me. I live to serve my Lord, to bear witness to him with word, song, and deeds. I'm sure I don't do as well as I should, but I am trying. I sing and my wife plays piano. When people call on us to perform it is a privilege to sing praises to God. The Lord has prospered me so well that I gladly do anything I can to witness and help others as much as I can.

Q: *What do you believe are the most important values to uphold and promote?*

A: Again, the Golden Rule, not only in your religious and personal life but also in business. I believe in total and complete honesty. I also believe we need to be very considerate of other people's feelings and show others respect. I remember when we were children and sold vegetables

7

from house to house, whenever the door was answered we always removed our headwear and greeted with a hello. To this day when I go to an office to talk with a lady, I always remove my hat. And if I meet a quite elderly lady on the street, I tip my hat to her. It's just simple respect and discipline.

Q: *What has given you the most joy in your life?*

A: Serving Jesus and helping others has given me the most joy. I also was very satisfied when the NAACP asked me to form a committee in South Dakota to help defeat the poll tax which kept poor people from voting, and our efforts were successful. Living here in Yankton I have had many opportunities that an African-American may not have had in other areas of the country. I have belonged to many civic organizations and in some cases been among the first Black people in the nation to be an officer in some of these groups. I have been blessed with many good friends.

Q: *What has given you the most sorrow in your life?*

A: In 1981 my first wife passed on. She had five and a half months between finding out she had cancer and her death. In that time she let me know she was confident that she was going to a wonderful new life. So even in the great sorrow of her death was the comfort of the Lord.

Q: *What are your hopes for the future?*

A: I hope we can strengthen the family and the home. I hope people can return to families that spend time together, that eat together and pray together. Many people want too much in material things and too little in real family unity. Some people seem too busy trying to impress their neighbors when they should be trying to impress their children. We need real homes for our children — homes of care, love, and discipline. If you bring up a child in the way you should, when he's old enough to go out on his own, things will be all right.

Q: *If there was one thing you could communicate to youth, what would it be?*

A: I would like young people to understand that their dreams for the future are important — that they can have their own vision and follow it. We cannot lose any more generations of our young people to crime, sex, and drugs. We must help them to a better life.

"When you wear eagle feathers you have to respect yourself and respect others. When you wear the feathers you have to encourage others, you have to share with and love others."
— *Steve Charging Eagle*

STEVE CHARGING EAGLE
born 1922

Steve Charging Eagle is a Lakota who was born, raised, and has lived his life along the Cherry Creek of the Cheyenne River Reservation in South Dakota. For fifty years he raised cattle and worked a variety of jobs on the reservation. Mr. Charging Eagle is an active member of the United Church of Christ and also follows the ways of Traditional Native American Religion.

Question: *What is your spiritual tradition and how does it form a foundation for your life?*

Answer: I believe in the Church and I believe in the Pipe. I pray in the Indian way and I pray in the Christian way; but I pray to the same God. There is only one God. We are all created by God.

Q: *How has your religion and religious practice given meaning to your life?*

A: I pray every morning, and I don't need a big church or a big Indian ceremony. I can be here in my house or out on a hill. What counts is what is in your heart. The prayer must be from your heart. God knows before you say anything. I am asked to do many naming ceremonies for families, where the child is given their Indian name. It is like a baptism. I do the ceremony of the six directions and the blessing of the feathers. The new name I choose comes from the deeds of two or three generations back in the child's family. The most important thing of the ceremony is the prayer. The prayer must come from the heart. I believe the Bible when it says "Work without faith is dead; and faith without work is dead." Ceremony and Church are both like this. You need the faith but you need to work at it and be honest about it.

Q: *What do you believe are the most important values to uphold and promote?*

A: I have been dancing with eagle feathers for thirty-five years. When I was a child, at my first naming ceremony my dad and uncle gave away six head of horses. In the second year when they blessed my feathers they gave away four more horses. Ten horses were given away over my feathers. That is why I am not afraid to wear eagle feathers. When you wear eagle feathers you have to respect yourself and respect others. When you wear the feathers you have to encourage others, you have to share with and love others. When I received the feathers as a boy an old man told me these things. My dad and uncle sometimes reminded me of these things. I didn't really understand as a kid, but I remembered them. When I was forty years old and started dancing I started wearing those feathers and I remembered. Now when I dance all those things come back to me.

Q: *What has given you the most joy in your life?*

A: Our five college-educated children and now our grandchildren give us great joy, and we take joy in honoring them. Our children recently greatly honored my wife and I on our forty-fifth wedding anniversary. They had a ceremony, a big dinner, a give away, a pow wow, and a dance contest for us. Our marriage was blessed by the Lakota Calf Pipe Carrier and in the Christian way by our oldest son who is a Reverend. We are very thankful to our children — we love them all. I also get much happiness from dancing at pow wows and all the friends we have made all over the country. I have been fortunate to have won many prizes for my dancing over the years, and when I do I always give part of the money to the church or to ceremonies. The Bible says that what you give comes back to you manyfold. That's true; it has always been that way for me. I spent ten years riding in the rodeo, I sang for years with a quartet in church; now I sing honor songs. All these things make me happy.

Q: *What has given you the most sorrow in your life?*

A: When I was two and a half years old my mother died and my father and uncle raised me. On Mother's Day even today, I remember her and wonder what she looked like and what kind of woman she was. The love and care of a mother I missed in my life. It is a sorrow I still feel in my heart. That is one of the reasons I keep going to church. I hope to see her someday.

Q: *What are your hopes for the future?*

A: I hope we live long enough to see our grandchildren graduate and get a good start in life. I hope this land I cared for all my life will stay in the family. My sons are going to take it after me, and I hope my grandsons will after them.

Q: *If there was one thing you could communicate to youth, what would it be?*

A: I worked with a shovel. I herded sheep and worked on horseback all day. Those times are gone. Now the people need a college education. That is something that they will always have. No one can take it away. They need to respect themselves and respect their teachers. I hope the Lakota people will keep their culture and keep their language. God gave us the Lakota language and we should not let it go. Wherever we go we will still be Indian, and I'm proud that I'm Indian.

"Christ had no desire for personal ownership, and I don't either. We have very nice homes to live in, we have plenty of food to eat, and we work very hard for our living, but we believe in sharing totally."
— *Henry Decker*

HENRY DECKER
born 1941

*Henry Decker is a member of the Pembrook Hutterite commu-
nity south of Ipswich, South Dakota. He was an educator of
the community's children for over a decade and is now the
group's business manager.*

Question: *What is your spiritual tradition and how does it
form a foundation for your life?*

Answer: The Hutterites trace their beginnings to the
Reformation, but they also differed from Martin Luther in
that they did not believe in the practices of child baptism
and communion. We have based our religion on the
teaching of Christ and in particular the book of Acts in
the New Testament. We believe in practicing the community of goods as well as we can possibly do it. Having
grown up in a Hutterite society, I do not want to own
things. Christ had no desire for personal ownership, and
I don't either. We have very nice homes to live in, we have
plenty of food to eat, and we work very hard for our living,
but we believe in sharing totally. I own nothing but my
clothes, and they were given to me by the community. We
work for posterity. We are here for our children to have a
home. I'm not working for myself, because when I go I will
take nothing and leave nothing in the way of worldly
goods. Our community is a corporation, and we pay reg-
ular corporate taxes to the state and federal governments.
We feel obligated to pay our share for the services we
receive. All Hutterite communities do this. We are pil-
grims here on this earth as far as God is concerned. We
believe we are here for a chance to get to heaven; that
goes for us in the Hutterite communities and for all those
living in other types of communities. As Hutterites we feel
we are doing what God wants us to do. Others may certainly do what they feel is the best way of life for them.
The door is always open in our community. Anyone may

15

leave at any time, and those may come that can live by the rules of our forefathers.

Q: *How has your religion and religious practice given meaning to your life?*

A: My religious experience gives me a sense of positive feelings. I try to live as well as possible the way Christ taught us and is teaching us. In the Old Testament God told Moses to teach the children every day. That is what we try to do every day with our children. We teach the German language and our religion together to our children.

Q: *What has given you the most joy in your life?*

A: The most joy comes from being put to the test every day and being able to take and stand the test. The only thing that has given me the necessary spiritual strength is the fact that I have a good family. My immediate family and many members of the community are my strength, and without them I know I would break down at times because the tests are very difficult. Helping each other out keeps me going. And, of course, the joy and strength of prayer are foundations in my life.

Q: *What has given you the most sorrow in your life?*

A: The most sorrow in my life comes from the fact that everyone does not live by our way of life both in our community and outside our community. Everyone wants to do their own thing. In our way of life that is not the way to live. When we need to do something in our society, even small things like going to town for supplies, we have to consult with others; it is the way we live — we live as a group.

Q: *What are your hopes for the future?*

A: My hope is for us to become better in our way of life. I hope we can be sounder and more stable. I hope we can build stronger constitutions in our hearts. The example we set for our young people today is what will be in the future.

Q: *If there was one thing you could communicate to youth, what would it be?*

A: To youth outside our community, I would like them to understand we are people like everyone else. We were put here by God for the same reason everyone else was. I hope people won't jump to conclusions about us and believe rumors about who we are. To our youth I would like to say that we need to educate the outside world on who we are. We are in a cocoon too much; we need to tell people what our purpose is here.

"God is not our servant, we are God's servants. Christianity has taught me to be tolerant. We need to love one another and look for similarities."
— *Aaron Glanzer*

AARON GLANZER
born 1927

Aaron Glanzer farmed in the Freeman, South Dakota area for forty years and is now retired and serving on several regional and international cooperative farming boards. He is a life-long member of the Mennonite faith.

Question: *What is your spiritual tradition and how does it form a foundation for your life?*

Answer: Martin Luther made the break with the Catholic Church. This led to the development that every person could have direct communication with God with no need for a church hierarchy. This was good but the emphasis on the individual weakened the good points of communal responsibilities and faith. Mennonites tried to develop a faith that balanced the individual and the community. We have a congregational form of church governing. We have no church hierarchy. My local church can do pretty much what it wants to. This gives us the potential to become who we think we are. It also gives us the responsibility to form a fellowship of believers to reach group consensus. This also led to fragmentation in the Mennonites with many different branches. There are now attempts to merge some of these factions. We are a pacifist people who believe in non-violence. We believe that Christ is the Son of God and He became human and died to liberate us from our guilt consciousness and set us free to live the abundant life. Christ is the foundation and we believe very strongly that works and faith need to go together. You can't separate the two, if you believe you must follow the teachings of Christ, and we take these teachings quite literally. The uniqueness of the Christian faith is that we believe Christ rose from the dead. Because of that I believe there is life after death. With that belief I can face the future and I don't have to worry. All things will eventually turn out for the good.

Q: *How has your religion and religious practice given meaning to your life?*

A: Attempting to live the teachings of Christ gives meaning to my life. If I can help someone else who needs help in any small way, I feel fulfilled. I have become very involved in our church on all levels of lay service. This involvement gives me much pleasure and satisfaction. I feel God has put into motion natural laws. We will reap what we sow. If I plant corn, I will harvest corn. If we as a culture plant violence in our society through our entertainment, we will reap violence through our children. We must learn to work for the best interest of humanity, not us, not the U.S., but work for the good of all — all are God's people. We must also learn to become true stewards of the land. The land does not belong to us. It belongs to God and we must do our best to care for it.

Q: *What do you believe are the most important values to uphold and promote?*

A: We need to remember that we have a vertical relationship with God. Some people see God as someone to fill their needs, to ask things from. God is sometimes seen as someone to fit into their agenda. God is not our servant, we are God's servants. Christianity has taught me to be tolerant. We need to love one another and look for similarities. As Mennonites, we believe in peace beyond simply resisting against war. We believe that peace is important in the church, the community, and in the home. We need to do everything in our power to get along with people even if it means being abused at times. You can't simply refuse to go in the army and still fight with your neighbor, for that is not consistent. My faith means I have to try to be consistent in who I am and how I treat others. I am far from perfect and I fall often, but I must try. The Bible and Mennonite history show us how much people of faith have suffered for their beliefs in the past and how imperfect we have been in our faith.

Q: *What has given you the most joy in your life?*

A: My family has given me much joy. Farming and my work with the church has also been very rewarding. I enjoy working with people and working with cooperatives.

Q: *What has given you the most sorrow in your life?*

A: There are many injustices around us that hurt people. The one that gives me the most pain is spouse and child abuse. To see taken away what is sacred in a child gives me deep sorrow.

Q: *What are your hopes for the future?*

A: The future for Christians is bright. My faith tells me that no matter what happens, God is in control. The body may be destroyed, but never the spirit. We need to change things we can change and to accept things we can't change. Historically the Christian Church has been the strongest when persecuted.

Q: *If there was one thing you could communicate to youth, what would it be?*

A: I hope young people will sit down and put down on paper what is really important to them — write a mission statement as to what you want your life to be. Then set your own agenda. Don't let your job or business tell you how to live your life. If you say your family is important, then be sure not to neglect them. If you say your church is important, then get involved in it. Don't let others set your agenda for you; it will only lead to unhappiness. The Christian faith has many opportunities for young people to build satisfying and productive lives.

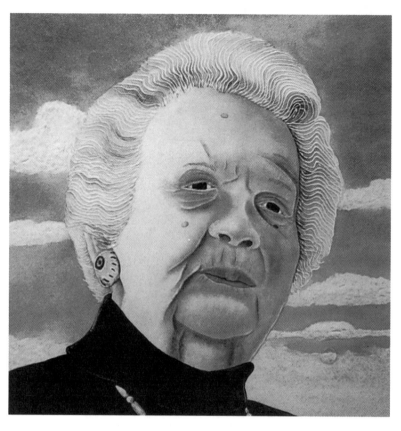

"I hope that through education we can learn to appreciate and respect our differences. I hope we can learn to respect and care for our environment. Peace on earth is one of my strongest hopes for the future. "
— *Esther Burnett Horne*

ESTHER BURNETT HORNE
born 1909

Esther Burnett Horne is an Eastern Shoshone who follows both the Episcopal and Traditional Native American faiths. She taught for over thirty years at the Wahpeton Indian School and is now retired, dividing her time between Wahpeton, North Dakota, and Naytahwaush, Minnesota on the White Earth Reservation.

Question: *What is your spiritual tradition and how does it form a foundation for your life?*

Answer: I feel very comfortable in both my religious traditions. Embracing both Christianity and Traditional Native American religion gives me a greater spiritual strength. There are many more similarities than differences in the faiths. The parallels are many, if you take the ten commandments and compare them with traditional Indian values, they match very well. I feel calm, serene, and peaceful with my religious beliefs. I rarely feel troubled; I have both my faiths to draw on. I may pray with an eagle feather, a pipe, a Christian prayer book, or while I am looking out the kitchen window. I have God and the Great Spirit to call on for answers to my prayers. I feel they are one and the same.

Q: *How has your religion and religious practice given meaning to your life?*

A: All in creation is a gift of Mother Earth. All my friends and relatives (and by relatives I mean everybody — we are all related) are all interdependent on one another. This is part of the tradition of the Native American and it gives my life deep meaning. This connectedness I feel from my Native American roots also extends and helps my relationship to my Episcopal faith as well. They are also my church family.

Q: *What do you believe are the most important values to uphold and promote?*

A: The value of bravery was needed in the last century when we were being moved from our lands. Today bravery means being brave enough to be your own person and not follow the crowd. People must be brave enough to leave drugs and alcohol alone; one must be able to overcome the negative inclinations within. Other important values are to respect the elders, to care for the environment, and individual freedom. By individual freedom I mean the freedom to care and work for the entire group. Recently I have been losing many of my dear friends and I was grieving and becoming depressed. I went to a non-Indian support group structured to assist those experiencing the loss of loved ones and it was a great help. This is what we Indian people have always done in most of our tribal groups. I'm glad we are getting back to this kind of group caring among all people. Another value important to me is generosity and sharing. Indian people have been criticized for their generosity. It is difficult for some to understand that friendship, family, and honor have greater value than material things. Another important value is to have respect for our brother's vision. By that I mean have respect for others' ideas and learn from them. And I have found that it doesn't make any difference how old you are, you can always learn.

Q: *What has given you the most joy in your life?*

A: My immediate family; my husband, children, grandchildren, and great grandchildren — other relatives and friends have given me great joy. Another wonderful joy of life was teaching. It was great to be paid for doing something that I loved to do. I truly love working with children. I started the first Indian Girl Scout troop in the United States because my great great grandmother, Sacajawea, was selected as their role model and was emblematic of their motto, "Be Prepared." I organized an "Indian Club" at the Wahpeton Indian School fifty-three years ago as a means of giving young Indian people a feeling of dignity and worth as individuals and a pride in their heritage. Since my retirement I have continued working with many groups of young people.

Q: *What has given you the most sorrow in your life?*

A: The deaths of my husband, my great grandson, Jordan, and my son-in-law, Bill Barney, have given me deep sorrow. Another great sorrow is when I study and reflect on the historical treatment of the Native American people. The most graphic example, I believe, is the Trail of Tears. I agonize over the ills that have been visited upon my people on the reservations by alcohol and drugs.

Q: *What are your hopes for the future?*

A: Even with our knowledge of the past, our attitude for the future must be positive. I had two very dedicated Native American women teachers at Haskell in the 1920's, Ella Deloria and Ruth Muskrat Bronson. I revered both of them. They became my role models. Both of them taught me pride in my Indianness, goodwill toward all races, and the importance of a positive attitude. They taught me that if you are carrying a chip on your shoulder you can always find someone to knock it off. I hope that through education we can learn to appreciate and respect our differences. I hope we can learn to respect and care for our environment. Peace on earth is one of my strongest hopes for the future.

Q: *If there was one thing you could communicate to youth, what would it be?*

A: We give lip service both in the Christian and Native American faiths to caring for one another: be your "brother's keeper." At the powwow you see the flag with the four colors representing all races of man. We need to truly respect our brothers' and sisters' visions. This means people of all races. Develop a healthy attitude.

"We are individuals but we are also members of this society and we must gauge our lives not only to satisfy ourselves but also to help, serve, and love others."
— *Sister Marie Kranz*

SISTER MARIE KRANZ
born 1919

Sister Marie Kranz has been a member of the Benedictine Order of Mount Marty since 1943. She has spent her life learning and teaching and is now working in the Learning Resource Center at Mount Marty College in Yankton, South Dakota.

Question: *What is your spiritual tradition and how does it form a foundation for your life?*

Answer: It has been basic. I went to Benedictine boarding school as a child and I am very grateful for the experience. I learned many marvelous things from the Benedictines; among those things was structure with flexibility — the idea of being firm but also being kind. I have appreciated that structure all my life; I am very much at home with Benedictine life. This form of value judgment and balance — the balance of the angelic and animal in ourselves — keeps us human. Benedictine structure has much to offer present day life. Distribution in the Benedictine way is according to need. Even the origin of the Order in the Sixth Century was a very democratic organization. In our Order even the young ones are listened to and people come together to make decisions. The final decision lies with the authority of the abbot or prioress, but not until he/she has carefully listened to others. Our life is based on scripture; we live out the Gospel message. We work for a clarification between our wants and our needs and take direction from that.

Q: *How has your religion and religious practice given meaning to your life?*

A: My practice has given a depth of meaning to my life. It has also given me pain in that I have observed others who feel alienated, alone, and suicidal. These are people who don't realize how much God loves them. This is a true tragedy in life, to go through life not knowing of God's love or even hating God due to warped and distorted ideas. We need to love God, love ourselves, and love others. The

Benedictine way is a reverence for life and for all things. Even the pots and pans of our kitchen have to be used as if they were sacred vessels of the altar. We have respect for things. The waste of the modern society is very painful to us. There are so many creative ways to use what some people think of as waste.

Q: *What do you believe are the most important values to uphold and promote?*

A: The value of the family; the breakdown of the family in recent decades has been a tragedy for the children of our society. I am afraid we are losing the art of parenting; true motherhood and fatherhood seem to be diminishing. Abortion, absent fathers, and a lack of accountability have led to a crisis in so many people's lives. There seems to be so few positive role models for young people to turn to. The current emphasis on greed and sex seem to permeate every problem we face.

Q: *What has given you the most joy in your life?*

A: The Lord has given me wonderful friends. My family, friends, and the monastic community have all given me great joy. I am grateful to the wonderful teachers I have had. Learning has given me much joy in my life as has teaching.

Q: *What has given you the most sorrow in your life?*

A: I was brought up in a family of seven girls and two boys in the depth of the Depression. We were materially poor but learned to be resourceful and do the best we could with what we had. We were very rich in our family life. Our values were strong. To see the collapse of the family and fading away of large families is painful to me. Another very current sorrow is to see the growth of gambling in our region and the governmental involvement in its promotion. We are closing schools and building more prisons. These are signs that something is wrong.

Q: *What are your hopes for the future?*

A: I hope people can come to know how wonderful they are, what a great gift they are to themselves and to each other. I hope people can come to understand that God loves them regardless of who they are. It is an unconditional love. This is the message of the Gospels. The scriptures are a book of love. We need to work for understanding, not always agreement but an understanding of one another. The greatest mystery is that of the Holy Trinity. The Holy Spirit speaks to people in many ways. We seem to be suffering from a lack of understanding of what authority really is. I believe that all authority comes from God and is delegated to us. It is a paradox that in finding true authority we also find true freedom. Extreme individualism and superficial sentimentality fight this realization. We are individuals but we are also members of this society and we must gauge our lives not only to satisfy ourselves but also to help, serve, and love others. Sentimentality can be a way to pay lip service to caring but never to penetrate true understanding and sacrifice.

Q: *If there was one thing you could communicate to youth, what would it be?*

A: I would like young people to know how much God loves them just the way they are. When they understand God's love they will naturally know how to make the necessary changes. God will take care of it from there. The complex problems around us are reduced to the simple when we listen to God. The power of God can either transcend our problems or solve them. But in this simplicity is mystery — the mystery of suffering, the mystery of love, the mystery of freedom. There is a transcendent capacity within us that moves us beyond words. Part of that power is pure belief. This power moves us beyond theories and words to a practical part of our lives and shapes the way we live. This mystery moves us away from alienation and loneliness to compassionate lives. It has been said that in the area of true belief no explanation is necessary and in the area of closed-minded disbelief, no explanation is possible.

"In Western culture there is much talk of 'I,' in Lakota culture it is 'We.' I cannot get ahead of my brother. We must go as a group."
— *Fred Leader Charge*

FRED LEADER CHARGE
born 1933

Fred Leader Charge was raised in the Parmalee area of the Rosebud Reservation in South Dakota. He was sent to Catholic and government boarding schools for his education. He received his higher education at Sinte Gleska University in Mission where he is now the Director of Student Support Services. Mr. Leader Charge follows the traditional Lakota religion.

Question: *What is your spiritual tradition and how does it form a foundation for your life?*

Answer: The Lakota religion is a way of life. It is a way to create a road, a way of good behavior, a way to deal with the bad we all encounter in life. When we go into the sweat lodge we take the bad with us and leave it there. The sweat is a physical and mental cleansing. In the sweat lodge the group becomes one. All pray for good health and help. What white people call a medicine man is really an interpreter. He thinks of himself as no better or more special than anyone else. He is the one to set the example of humility. Now we have a lot of "plastic" medicine men who do ceremonies for money. You can't put religion on the auction block. You can't sell culture; it belongs to the people. In the old days only four or five men participated in the Sun Dance, now dozens and dozens dance. In the old days those who danced were very good people willing to make the sacrifice for good health and help to those in need. We believe that all we own is our bodies, so when we want to make a special sacrifice to help others it is our bodies that we give in the Sun Dance. In those days the Sun Dance was for the health and survival of the people.

Q: *How has religion given meaning to your life?*

A: God is not something specific; it is everything. All creation is the Creator. The animals, the grass, the trees, the water, you, me, we are all parts of the Creator. Another important component to the meaning in the Lakota reli-

31

gion is that of our language and our songs. The ceremonial songs are very important and deeply meaningful. They can be songs that honor or songs that mourn. They are songs that help people in many ways. It is only through the Lakota language that these songs can bring their meaning, healing, and hope to the people.

Q: *What do you believe are the most important values to uphold and promote?*

A: The kinship system is at the heart of Lakota values. The kinship system is based on how you react to people around you. Everyone and everything is related to you. In the kinship system you have set ways of behavior. You have a way to talk to your mother and a way to talk to your father. There is a way to relate to all your relatives. It is based on mutual respect. If we lose this, our culture will be gone. My father's brothers are also my fathers, my mother's sisters are also my mothers; the kinship system creates a fabric of belonging. It holds the Lakota culture together. In Western culture there is much talk of "I," in Lakota culture it is "We." I cannot get ahead of my brother. We must go as a group. There is much in traditional Lakota values that goes against the grain of Western individualism, competitiveness, and ownership. How can land belong to me when it is me that belongs to the land? All the other Lakota values such as generosity, bravery, wisdom, and respect grow from this kinship system. Today there is much lip-service to these values, but it must go beyond talk; you have to live the values. They can't be forced on young people. Values and traditions must be learned from example and become a natural, automatic way of life. This is very difficult when so many Indian people have one foot in the white world and one foot in the Indian world.

Q: *What has given you the most joy in your life?*

A: My family. My wife and I raised six children and we are now raising four of our grandchildren. We have the advantage now of knowing the mistakes we made with our children so we can do a better job with the grandchildren. We are, as all grandparents do, also spoiling them.

Q: *What has given you the most sorrow in your life?*

A: One of our grandchildren was killed by a drunk driver. The driver was a white rancher who never spent a day in jail.

Q: *What are your hopes for the future?*

A: We need a new awareness that assimilation and acculturation has occurred. We have trivialized, commercialized, and exploited our cultural heritage, meaning ceremonies, etc. Erosion of the culture is evident. An example is the pow wow. It was a social event that involved giveaways and dancing. Today anyone can look to any major city and the pow wow is commercialized with big prize money for dancing. Another aspect that relates to the future is that it is very hard for people to see that we are all one. But we must come to understand this. Man is the most violent and destructive creature on this earth. If man doesn't wake up soon, we may not be here much longer.

Q: *If there was one thing you could communicate to youth, what would it be?*

A: Education. Through education we can gain more understanding, through understanding maybe wisdom. Both my fathers still call me the Lakota name for boy when they greet me. I have not yet gained the wisdom to be called the Lakota name for Man. In my way of thinking I see myself as a common man, nothing special. When we go into a ceremony we present ourselves to the Creator as a common man — that's all we are. Addendum: IKE WISCASA CONALA OKIYA PI BLE HI CA YA PO. LACOL OWATE! (Common man is on the decline — be brave Lakotas.)

"The Christian beatitudes are a good guide to values. One should strive to be ethical, honest, kind, compassionate, and humble. Many religions have much we can learn about values and morals."

— *Winifred Brown Lee*

Winifred Brown Lee
born 1912

Winifred Brown Lee was a teacher in 1930's, 1940's, and 1950's. She then raised a family and is now retired in Sioux Falls, South Dakota. She is a member of the Unitarian-Universalist Church.

Question: *What is your spiritual tradition and how does it form a foundation for your life?*

Answer: I grew up in a liberal Presbyterian Church. My mother was a member and my father attended services whenever one of the children took part. On Easter Sunday, when I was fourteen years old I was baptized, joined the church, and gave the program during Sunday school. Before joining I was questioned as to what I would do in a time of crisis, and I replied I would consult my conscience. The excellent Sunday school orchestra and church choir in which I participated held my interest through high school and college. But with college and my exposure to free-thinking professors, I began to feel uncomfortable with the Presbyterian dogma. I taught for a year at Oglala Community High School and became keenly aware of the cruel way in which Christian missionaries, including Presbyterians, had stifled the beautiful, sensible religion of the Oglala Lakota. I quietly joined the Church of the Larger Fellowship, a niche for Unitarians who have no church in their community. About twenty-two years ago I joined the Unitarian-Universalist fellowship in Sioux Falls. I had long been familiar with and admired great people such as Joseph Priestly, Thomas Jefferson, Louisa Alcott, Susan Anthony, and Clara Barton, not realizing that they were Unitarians or Universalists. (The two groups merged in 1961.) I feel at home in the non-creedal Unitarian-Universalist Church as I do not believe in a literal interpretation of the Bible. I believe there are common threads in the beliefs and scriptures of all the major religions of the world and many paths in one's search for the truth. I reject the doctrine of the Trinity and see no sense in worrying about Hell. Why not alleviate misery in the here and now? I think Jesus was a good person but on Easter I believe in emphasizing the rebirth of Nature over the Resurrection story. To me religion is a search for the meaning of life, and I hope there is a spark of divinity in each human. I believe what I must after careful scrutiny and prayerful analysis. At present I am a humanist gaining support from friends instead of a nebulous God (or Goddess).

Q: *What do you believe are the most important values to uphold and promote?*

A: I believe that principles of justice and truth are very important. The Christian beatitudes are a good guide to values. One should strive to be ethical, honest, kind, compassionate, and humble. Many religions have much we can learn about values and morals.

Q: *What has given you the most joy in your life?*

A: My greatest joy is when a great-grandchild climbs on my lap and asks me to read a story. Another joy is to have one of my former students remember me and thank me for the difficulties I gave them — they can appreciate it now!

Q: *What has given you the most sorrow in your life?*

A: Some of our relatives could not accept the bi-racial children my husband and I adopted; that was a great sorrow to me.

Q: *What are your hopes for the future?*

A: One of my hopes for the future is that some day we will see an end to discrimination against minorities, homosexuals, and women.

Q: *If there was one thing you could communicate to youth, what would it be?*

A: I would like to tell them to keep a sense of humor and to be flexible. They are growing up in a time of very rapid technological change and young people will need to be able to be adaptable.

"One of my old uncles once told me a Lakota prophecy that Mother Earth is going to wash herself. That's what is happening now and if we don't pray it may just wash us all down to the Gulf."

— *Ollie Napesni*

OLLIE NAPESNI
born 1917

Ollie Napesni was born in a tent at St. Francis on the Rosebud Reservation in South Dakota. She grew up on Rosebud and left the state in 1940 to return again in 1961. She has been an educator for the past twenty-five years, teaching from the lower grades to higher education as a language and traditional arts teacher at Sinte Gleska University in Mission. She now is semi-retired. Ms. Napesni, who was raised in the Catholic faith, is now a follower of traditional Lakota religion.

Question: *What is your spiritual tradition and how does it form a foundation for your life?*

Answer: I went to St. Francis Boarding School where we went to church every day and three times on Sunday. It was pray, pray, pray. I figure I did enough Christian praying in those days to last a lifetime. After I was married I became very ill with gall stones and the doctors couldn't do anything to help me. My husband convinced me to see a traditional medicine man who gave medicine and performed a ceremony and I came out of there well. That was after being on a liquid diet for six months. I was nothing but a living skeleton. We then moved out of the state but that experience really kindled my interest in the traditional ways. I came to realize that I knew nothing of my people's traditional ways or history. We were taught nothing in school. When living in Denver I began going to the library and reading books on Indian culture. I read and read. I also began having dreams of a sweat lodge even though I had never been to a sweat lodge or seen one. After we returned to Rosebud I began learning more and following the traditional religion of my people. In 1964 I started to Sun Dance.

Q: *What do you believe are the most important values to uphold and promote?*

A: I believe we must bring back, preserve, and use our Lakota language. The language is necessary to understand our values. A real understanding of Lakota traditions and values cannot be gained without the language that can fully express them. When I teach language courses, history and culture are an important and popular part of my teaching.

Q: *What has given you the most joy in your life?*

A: Having my children. I have two daughters who gave me seven grandchildren, who have now given me two great-grandchildren. I also adopted two sons and a non-Indian daughter. I have six grandchildren from them.

Q: *What has given you the most sorrow in your life?*

A: In 1993 my son was accompanying me to a conference in Rapid City. The last evening of the conference he was abducted and brutally murdered. The trial of the three killers took a year and there is still talk of appeals. I have never been the same and will never be the same as before. I have not been able to participate in ceremonies because my heart has been full of sorrow and anger. I recently have had dreams of my son that may be telling me it is time to return to the ceremonies.

Q: *What are your hopes for the future?*

A: One of my old uncles once told me a Lakota prophecy that Mother Earth is going to wash herself. That's what is happening now and if we don't pray it may just wash us all down to the Gulf. My dad gave me eighty acres of land and told me to hang on to it because hard times were coming. Hard times are here. There are so few full-bloods and elders left to teach the people. Alcohol has gotten a hold on so many of our people. Now the casinos — they may be the final destruction for our people. Money now controls many people. There are people who have given up all hope. I have good children and their families; I have hopes for them.

Q: *If there was one thing you could communicate to youth, what would it be?*

A: When I talk to young children I always tell them what my Dad told me when I was a young girl. He said, "Get up early, don't sleep late, see that sun rise every morning, that sun is our life." To this day I get up at 4:00 every morning and go to bed at 8:30 in the evening. You can get a lot done in a day if you get up early. He also said, "Take care of your body, be careful of what you put in your body. There are bad things coming in the future. Keep your body clean by the way you live." He also said "Listen to your Mom. Even if you don't agree, don't answer back at her — she's your Mom." Everyday I would hear these things from my Dad until they became a natural way of life. When I talk to older children and teenagers I tell them not to let that television control them. Don't try to look like the people on TV; you are an Indian and you should be proud. Dress simply and look like an Indian. Now, I also tell the older ones about the murder of my son. They see so much violent entertainment they need to know violence is real and can happen to anyone. You have to be very careful and take care of yourself.

"Our religious responsibility includes Tikkun Olam, repairing the world. We human beings are incomplete creatures and we must try to finish ourselves. We can't wait around for God to do it for us."

— *Gail Pickus*

GAIL PICKUS
born 1934

Gail Pickus was born and raised in the Jewish faith in Chicago, Illinois. She moved to Aberdeen, South Dakota, with her husband in 1954 and has raised a family of three sons. She is a visual artist and active in many aspects of the Aberdeen community.

Question: *What is your spiritual tradition and how does it form a foundation for your life?*

Answer: All of my grandparents and my Dad were immigrants from Russia. My maternal grandfather left Telz, Russia and orthodox Judaism in 1888 when he came to this country. Eventually settling in Chicago, he was one of the organizers of the reform Temple Judea founded in 1914 to counter the loss of orthodox practices. Growing up in the 1940's, I received a good basic education in the more middle-of-the road conservative branch of Judaism, learning Jewish history, customs, and Hebrew language at Sunday School. In my Chicago neighborhood I had plenty of company. Half my schoolmates were Jewish. I attended mainly Jewish camps and later became a counselor at one of them. When we moved to Aberdeen the situation was very different. In a community with few Jews you become more responsible for your own faith and for explaining it to your Sunday School children and to others outside the Jewish community. So over the years I have learned a lot about spiritual, cultural, and historic Judaism. Lately, I've even taken to quietly saying an appreciative Shehekyanu blessing thanking God for bringing me to any special moment. Literally, the blessing reads: "Praised are You, Lord our God, King of the universe, who has blessed us with life, sustained us, and enabled us to reach this season." Judaism is a spiritual aid but it also appeals to my sense of reason. Edmond Fleg has said, "I am a Jew because Judaism demands no abdication of my mind." I do a great deal of reading and asking questions such as, "Where was God during the

Holocaust?" For some, faith is enough. They say, "You don't question God. You can't question God's complexities." The more I read though, the more I think the Holocaust — any holocaust — is man's failure, not God's. Our religious responsibility includes Tikkun Olam, repairing the world. We human beings are incomplete creatures and we must try to finish ourselves. We can't wait around for God to do it for us. I don't think of God as watching each sparrow. There is plenty of sparrow-watching to go around for us all. Judaism is a religion with a rich, varied literary heritage. In the long history of these writings is a sense of openness that allows many points of view and an ability for Judaism to adapt itself to new historical and social circumstances. I have had Christian friends who have been worried that I won't be admitted to heaven. As with many Jews, I don't think much about heaven. I don't believe there is a set of exact rules one must follow to be with God. I believe we must try to make a good and caring life while we are here on earth. Judaism has given me the confidence to do what is necessary and a sense of comfort in the traditions of the faith. I've been to many Temples and Synagogues in my life-time and am most at home in our local Aberdeen Congregation B'Nai Isaac Synagogue, one of only two syna-gogues in the state of South Dakota. As Theodore Bikel described a similar synagogue, "where those Jews didn't need an interpreter to God, you know, one who could translate from English into Hebrew. They had their pipeline, each one of them, and they sang out of tune and beat their breasts and they were loud and they were my Jews."

Q: *How has your religion and religious practice given meaning to your life?*

A: Judaism is the underpinning of my life. It is so deeply con-nected to the family. The many holidays of Judaism are part of the bonding and the joy of this belonging. Holidays, holiday dinners, and ceremonies tie together the family and Jewish community and become a kind of core of life. Judaism is a home-based religion. In a small Jewish community as we have here, the entire group can fit into a family's living room. This also creates a sense of togetherness.

Q: *What do you believe are the most important values to uphold and promote?*

A: Do unto others as you would have them do unto you. Sam Levenson's four letter words: help, give, feel, care, and love are tenets to live by. I have no desire to change anyone. I would simply like to be helpful where and when I can.

Q: *What has given you the most joy in your life?*

A: Our children and now our grandchildren. It has been wonderful to watch them grow to be good people. Our children were fortunate to grow up with their grandparents, and I know as they helped us care for these same grandparents how they learned about the circle of life. Another great joy has been and continues to be learning. I try to absorb and use everything I can, and then I hope I can get a book on it.

Q: *What are your hopes for the future?*

A: We have much work to do. Charity needs to be both one to one and also charity with a global conscience. But peace must always start at home.

Q: *If there was one thing you could communicate to youth, what would it be?*

A: I would hope young people will learn as much as they can, taking advantage of knowledge from all sources. Sometimes even people who you might not especially like can teach you important things, and some of the best lessons are learned from mistakes. I would also counsel for patience, a positive outlook, and the ability to savor the moment. Lastly, remember that "morality, like art, consists of drawing the line somewhere."

"Faith gives people a real reason for living and with faith you can help people. Faith gives you the love for others that makes you want to help people whether they agree with you or not."

— *Harold E. Salem*

HAROLD E. SALEM
born 1921

Harold E. Salem has been a pastor in the American Baptist Churches USA, for fifty-one years. For the past thirty-seven years he has ministered to the members of the First Baptist Church in Aberdeen, South Dakota.

Question: *What is your spiritual tradition and how does it form a foundation for your life?*

Answer: All my life, my principles, my goals center in the Bible. I believe the Bible is divinely inspired and correct in every way. Interpreted correctly, it never contradicts itself. The spiritual is everything to me. As a matter of fact, the material world is really not that important. When you get older the material things don't have the shine they did when you were young.

Q: *How has your religion and religious practice given meaning to your life?*

A: Everything I have comes from and is based on my faith. Jesus is my Savior, my redeemer, my guide, and my model. How to serve him and honor him is the true meaning in life. I must be careful never to do anything that would desecrate the name of Christ or the Church. I would rather die than do that. My faith is everything to me; I don't have anything else. I love my family and my friends but even those relationships are based on the premise of how they relate to my faith.

Q: *What do you believe are the most important values to uphold and promote?*

A: People must put their faith in Jesus because I believe everyone has a soul, and that soul will be in heaven or hell forever. Faith gives people a real reason for living and with faith you can help people. Faith gives you the love for others that makes you want to help people whether they agree with you or not. Jesus has taught us that we must do good works, and not just talk. We must get out there and help people. My faith is to have people saved, or "born again." Love is unconditional whether you are my friend or my enemy. That is a hard lesson that Jesus taught.

Q: *What has given you the most joy in your life?*

A: The most joy in my life has come from giving people faith, to give them Christ in their lives. This faith can help people in all the times of life and especially the difficult times. In financial difficulty, sickness, divorce, and even death I have seen faith give them serenity, peace, and confidence. To see faith grow as a viable force in someone's life is my greatest joy.

Q: *What has given you the most sorrow in your life?*

A: I hate to see people hurting. Hunger, broken homes, divorces, young people throwing their lives away on drugs, liquor, and illicit sex, I feel bad about seeing those things. To see people reject Christ when he died for them and could do so much for them, that is the saddest thing.

Q: *What are your hopes for the future?*

A: With the Gospel there is always hope. It is a proclamation of hope. Education and wealth can't give real hope. You must have a relationship with Jesus Christ. Even with the great despair we see in the world, there is a bright side, and that's God's side. We need to look for the joy and meaning and purpose of life. That's what people want. There is a place in the hearts of men and women for God. Until they find Christ they will never be satisfied.

Q: *If there was one thing you could communicate to youth, what would it be?*

A: The youth need a personal relationship with Jesus. That's where you start, and then they need to know there is value in morals, in living a clean life. There is value in having goals and working hard. The soul has to be right with God first, and then you build on that. They need to understand that they are important to God and God loves them; there is work for them to do. Their lives make a difference in this society. Who knows how God will use them? I get encouragement from young people. They have a tough time in today's world but Christ can give them the strength to overcome. We need to fill our minds with the good things of God.

"It gives me a great deal of joy to assist people, whether it is as a mentor in a senior center or hugging a child in kindergarten. Love is a two-way street, what you give always comes back to you."
— *Grace Sanderson*

GRACE SANDERSON
born 1921

Grace Sanderson and her husband, Cecil, raised a family of seven boys and one girl. They lived in Sisseton, South Dakota for fifteen years before moving to Brookings County in 1960. She is now retired in Brookings but very active in church and community volunteer work. She is a life-long member of the Lutheran church.

Question: *What is your spiritual tradition and how does it form a foundation for your life?*

Answer: The way I was brought up by my parents was to be a caring and sharing person, following the teachings of Christ. I was taught a faith that assured me that all things will work for good. Agape love, self-sacrificing love, is an important part of this. I certainly don't know how all things work, but in the end everything comes out as God's will. My parent's were very religious and that was instilled in us. The church was the center of the community in those days. It was our social life as well as our religious life.

Q: *How has your religion and religious practice given meaning to your life?*

A: Jesus is a wonderful example of caring and sharing, and He is a good act to follow. In my life my husband and I have raised eight children and we certainly realize that life in not a bed of roses. There are always thorns along the way. The teachings of Jesus have created a meaningful way for us to live our lives and to give guidance to our children when these thorns were on our path. While there is no way we can actually be like Christ, he set a wonderful direction in which we can follow.

Q: *What do you believe are the most important values to uphold and promote?*

A: It is natural for those following Christ's example to promote and uphold what is good. If one truly cares for others it is natural to help them. Not because you are told to, but because it is fundamental to your behavior. It helps the receiver and it also helps the giver. All the important values come when you follow the path of Jesus. When we make mistakes we need to learn from those mistakes and carry on.

Q: *What has given you the most joy in your life?*

A: I enjoy sharing with others in whatever ways I can. I do a great deal of volunteer work with many organizations in the community. It gives me a great deal of joy to assist people, whether it is as a mentor in a senior center or hugging a child in kindergarten. Love is a two-way street, what you give always comes back to you. I was brought up in the 1930's when all we had to live on was the cream check, but I never felt deprived. We learned to work and we cared for one another. Joy doesn't come from what you have but from what you give.

Q: *What has given you the most sorrow in your life?*

A: I feel a great sorrow when I see people who have no respect for other people and their property. I was taught as a small child to always respect the property of others, and even what belonged to you was to be respected.

Q: *What are your hopes for the future?*

A: My highest hope is to see my grandchildren grow to be useful citizens. There is so much temptation for children now. It is a difficult time to grow-up.

Q: *If there was one thing you could communicate to youth, what would it be?*

A: The example of one's life should be the real message to young people. I hope the youth can develop respect for others and see the needs of others through following the example of Jesus.

"There needs to be more respect. People must respect one another. Children must respect and be obedient to their parents. It all needs to start at home. Parents need to teach their children values and prayer."
— *Geraldine Sherman*

GERALDINE SHERMAN
born 1922

Geraldine Sherman is a Lakota who was born and raised in Kyle, South Dakota. She attended government boarding school, married, and raised a family of eight children. Mrs. Sherman is now a seamstress and clothing designer living in Rapid City. She is a member of the Catholic church.

Question: *What is your spiritual tradition and how does it form a foundation for your life?*

Answer: My folks were not overly religious. In those days the government was suppressing traditional Indian religion. My mother was raised in a Catholic orphanage. When I was nine both my parents joined the Catholic church. We also went to local Lakota gatherings and celebrations where the prayer was said in Lakota but I had no idea what they were talking about. The Catholic church at that time was very strict about their members not participating in Indian religion. Now things are very different. Our Parish at times uses sage, the drum, the Lakota language, and other traditional aspects in the Catholic ceremonies. It is so much better this way. I believe the traditional Indian religion and the Catholic religion have much in common. I believe in the story of the White Buffalo Calf Woman. I believe it was the Virgin Mary teaching our people ways to live.

Q: *How has your religion and religious practice given meaning to your life?*

A: I have been very involved with our parish since my children were in their first Catechism classes. Many years ago we began a Blessed Kateri Tekawitha Circle and I have been president of the group twice. We try to send some of our members to the National Kateri Conference every year and we have just completed a fund raising drive to have a bronze statue of Blessed Kateri created for our Church. It is now completed and looks lovely in the Church. If it were not for my religion, I probably would have been insane years ago. One must have faith or we lose it all. I believe in prayer and miracles. I had to go through a divorce that was terrible for me. It was prayer that helped me through it. After that I was left with no support and it was a miracle that helped me develop a career as a clothing designer to have a livelihood for me and my family. Prayer helps in all things. For the past twelve years I have tried to attend Mass daily. It helps me so much to cope with and accept the negative things in life. I depend on God for everything. I see the beauty of God in all that is around me. I pray to Jesus, the Virgin, and Saints for their help in all aspects of my life.

Q: *What do you believe are the most important values to uphold and promote?*

A: There needs to be more respect. People must respect one another. Children must respect and be obedient to their parents. It all needs to start at home. Parents need to teach their children values and prayer. I think the TV is creating many problems with children. They watch so much violence. I think the problems of the family are reflected by many of the other problems we have in life. We need to get along.

Q: *What has given you the most joy in your life?*

A: My children and now my thirty-one grandchildren and great grandchildren. I am particularly proud of the education many of my children obtained. Some of my children who have pursued careers in education are teaching from pre-school to university levels. Some of my other children have pursued careers in various aspects of the construction industry. I am proud of them all.

Q: *What has given you the most sorrow in your life?*

A: My oldest girl developed rheumatoid arthritis when she was in Junior High and suffered with it the rest of her life. She was an educator and children loved her dearly. She died last year at the age of fifty of heart failure.

Q: *What are your hopes for the future?*

A: I have been blessed in that most of my children are doing very well, but there are problems I would like to see end. Alcohol has been a plague on my family and many other families. I pray the desire for alcohol will end. It will take a miracle, but I believe in miracles.

Q: *If there was one thing you could communicate to youth, what would it be?*

A: Religion has been everything to me. I hope young people will join a religion and learn to pray. You don't have to be perfect to pray. It is when you have problems that you need prayer and God the most. God loves everyone. We just need to ask for God's help.

"We need to try to care
and reach out to people in
need and distress. We need
to be more giving and not
worry so much about accu-
mulating wealth."
— *Harlan Stoley*

HARLAN STOLEY
born 1925

Harlan Stoley was born on the farm. For the past fifty years he has been farming north of Highmore, South Dakota. He has been a life-long member of the Lutheran church.

Question: *What is your spiritual tradition and how does it form a foundation for your life?*

Answer: I'm thankful to my grandfather and parents for impressing on me the importance of the Christian beliefs. I'm also thankful to the church for defending, preserving, and teaching the scriptures through the centuries. There are some frustrations in being a member of the organized church. We proclaim that Jesus is our king, but we don't always treat him like a king. We sometimes seem to think of Him as another member of a democracy who can easily be out-voted. Churches and church leaders need to truly emphasize the teaching of Jesus of Nazareth. We often say the right things but it is hard to get the congregation motivated to do the right things. The key in my faith journey comes from the story of the Transfiguration where the voice of God came from heaven and said, "This is My Son, My Beloved, listen to Him." We need to follow what He said, what His teachings are. That is not always easy, but we need to try to follow in His footsteps. Jesus was so compassionate, understanding, caring, and forgiving to all people. He created difficult footsteps to follow and I fail again and again. It is important to keep trying.

Q: *How has your religion and religious practice given meaning to your life?*

A: In trying to following the teachings of Christ I have become involved in the reconciliation efforts between Native Americans and whites in the state. It has been a way to try to take action rather than just talk about justice. It is a long, difficult process with much left to be done. In the twenty years I have been involved there has been some progress and some sliding backwards. In my everyday life I try to follow Christ's example of caring and forgiving. There is so much hatred expressed around us. I hope to contradict some of that thinking when possible.

Q: *What do you believe are the most important values to uphold and promote?*

A: We need to try to care and reach out to people in need and distress. We need to be more giving and not worry so much about accumulating wealth. Honesty and fairness are other important values, both in our personal lives and our business lives. Sometimes it is difficult to see what is fair. Sometimes we get caught in the middle of a situation, but we need to try our best.

Q: *What has given you the most joy in your life?*

A: I would have to put my family at the top. My wife is my partner and my best friend. We have five living daughters that have gone on to useful lives and given us a dozen grandkids. Another joy is all the wonderful people I have met from many religions who take their faith seriously. It has been a joy and inspiration to know them.

Q: *What has given you the most sorrow in your life?*

A: We had one daughter and son-in-law who were killed in a car accident. This great tragedy and all the consequences to their children and the entire family was a deep sorrow. Another great worry and pain to me is the continuing destruction of the family farm system by forty years of the government's cheap food policy. I have watched the suffering, pain, despair, depression, and destruction of many good friends who worked hard all their lives and lost everything when they were sixty-five years old. We almost went bankrupt a couple times ourselves but managed to survive. Many of our neighbors didn't. We can't help but share some of the pain with them. To see the family farm way of life coming to an end is a sad thing. Many of these farmers have developed a real bonding with the land.

Q: *What are your hopes for the future?*

A: I hope that somehow we can get more people back on the land in smaller units, the size that a family can care for. We always said that when we retire, as none of our daughters married farmers, we would sell our farm to a young family, but we can't. No young person could afford the interest rates, taxes, and overhead costs and still support a family. So our only choice is now to sell it to a big operation that would just absorb our farm. I still hope that there can be some ways to make it possible for smaller family farms to continue. I pray that urban people of all ages will come to realize, before it is too late, that they too are dependant on a gracious God, topsoil, and the people who live close to the land.

Q: *If there was one thing you could communicate to youth, what would it be?*

A: I hope that each young person could find a good relationship with God. Part of this relationship would be to learn to reach out to their fellow humans of the world regardless of race or creed. I hope they could have respect for the land and all creation. It does take time to reach this sense of a bond. I marvel at the beauty of the night sky and the variety of wildflowers on the prairie. There is joy in watching a deer and her fawn or sometimes a fox or coyote. The occupation of farming has built-in therapy. I hope young people will also have the opportunity to experience God's creation in this way.

Mark W. McGinnis is an artist and educator at Northern State University in Aberdeen, South Dakota. His interdisciplinary approach to art has included paintings, sculpture, collagraphs, installation, video, performance, essays, and interviews. The research orientation of his work has led to projects of exploration and inquiry on a range of subjects including religion, history, and explorers of the "New World."

McGinnis' projects have been featured in over seventy solo exhibitions nationwide. His publications include the 1994 book, *Lakota and Dakota Animal Wisdom Stories* and several articles in *The Chronicle of Higher Education.*

KEY TO COVER PORTRAITS

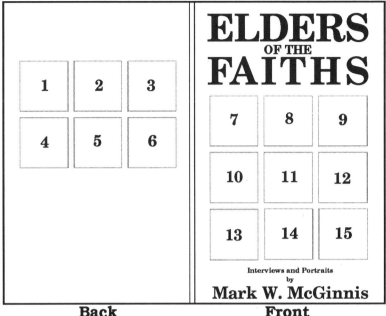

ELDERS
OF THE
FAITHS

7	8	9
10	11	12
13	14	15

Interviews and Portraits
by
Mark W. McGinnis

Back   Front

BACK:
1. Geraldine Sherman,
2. Beryl Blake,
3. Harlan Stoley,
4. Harold E. Salem,
5. Esther Burnett Horne,
6. Henry Decker.

FRONT:
7. Fred Leader Charge,
8. Aaron Glanzer,
9. Gail Pickus,
10. Grace Sanderson,
11. Ted Blakey,
12, Sister Marie Kranz,
13. Winifred Brown Lee,
14. Ollie Naspesni,
15. Steve Charging Eagle.

ORDER FORM:
ELDERS OF THE FAITHS
and other books from
EX MACHINA PUBLISHING CO.

__*Elders of the Faiths,* by Mark W. McGinnis,
@ 9.95 ea. $_____

__*The Forgotten People* (Das vergessene Volk)
A year among the Hutterites, by Michael
Holzach, Translated by Stephan Lhotzky,
Trade Paper back @ $14.95 ea. $_____
Hardbound @ $21.95 ea. $_____

__*Born Hutterite,* Stories by Samuel Hofer,
@ $10.95 ea. $_____
Three Audio Cassettes, Read By the Author,
@ $19.95 ea. set $_____

__*Dance like a Poor Man,* by Samuel Hofer,
@ $10.95 ea. $_____

__*The Hutterite Community Cookbook,* by
Samuel Hofer, @ $11.95 ea. $_____

SUBTOTAL $_____

In South Dakota add 4% Sales Tax $_____
In Sioux Falls add 6% Sales Tax $_____
Postage Paid by Publisher

PLEASE REMIT   TOTAL $_____

Name_____

Streeet Address_____

City_____State____Zip_____

Send Order To: EX MACHINA PUBLISHING CO.
Box 448
Sioux Falls, SD, 57101